My Time To Color

Libra Zodiac Sign

Coloring Book

Copyright 2017 –

Swift Publishing/MyTimeToColor.com

All Rights Reserved

Images May Not Be Replicated or Reproduced

Some design elements/images used under license from Shutterstock. Some design elements designed by Freepik from FlatIcon.com.

ISBN-13: 978-1977564733

ISBN-10: 1977564739

ZODIAC SUN SIGN LIBRA

September 24 to October 23   (* see following 'Born on the CUSP?')

Symbol: Scales

Element: Air

Quality: Cardinal

Ruling Planet: Venus

Lucky numbers: 5, 6, 9

Color: Blue

Favorite Environment: Social Activities

Governs: Lumbar, lower back, kidneys

Best Pet: Prue Breed

Flowers: Lilly, Rose

BORN ON THE CUSP?

Your zodiac sign is based upon the position of the Sun when you were born. At the time and place of your birth the Sun was in a specific position and therefore within a specific zodiac sign. While it would be more convenient if the Sun's transition from one sign to another happened exactly at midnight on any given day, it doesn't. Plus there are many various time zones throughout the world, so your midnight would not be the same as midnight for someone in a different time zone.

In addition, a calendar year is not the same as the Earth's annual revolution (circling) of the Sun. The actual length of a sidereal year (time required for Earth to revolve once around the Sun) is actually 365.25635 days. That is why every four years there is a leap year of 366 days to compensate for the error caused by the calendar year being shorter than the sidereal year.

This is why the Sun can be in different zodiac signs on the same calendar day in different years. The start and end dates of the zodiac signs can and do vary from year to year.

In reality the Sun was in one specific position, and therefore one specific sign, when you were born. Before the age of computers it used to be very time consuming to determine your sign if you were born on the cusp (near the beginning or end of a sign).

Now there are online calculators that you can use to make this determination. You will get the most accurate results if you have all three of these: 1) your day of birth 2) your time of birth and 3) your place of birth. Most calculators will still allow you to calculate your sun sign without your time of birth but the determination could be off. Input these three items into an accurate online sun sign calculator and you will be able to confidently determine your Sun sign.

This web page has an online calculator for determining your sign:
www.MyTimeToColor.com/sign

WHAT IS ASTROLOGY?

Astrology is the use of heavenly bodies to guide us in our lives. It is based on the belief that the stars and planets have a direct impact on our lives and that their relative positions to each other predict certain events. Most people know astrology from their horoscopes and some characteristics of their Zodiac sign, but there is much more to it. You can gain a deeper knowledge of astrology and use it to improve your life.

There are twelve Zodiac signs. Your day and time of your birth determines your zodiac sign. Each Zodiac sign also has a quality, an element, and a ruling planet (or two). For example, if you were born November 14th, (like me!) your sign is Scorpio, your element is Water, your quality is Fixed, and your ruling planets are Pluto and Mars. Each of these pieces of astrological information give you useful knowledge about yourself and how you will interact with people of different Zodiac signs.

History of Astrology

Astrology has a rich history and has arisen independently in many civilizations throughout the centuries. Ever since the rise of humans, people have been observing the stars and planets. Knowledge of these bodies increased drastically with writing to record patterns that took place over long periods of time. Astrology first originated with the Babylonians about 4,000 years ago, when they began to use the stars to predict seasonal and astronomical events.

Since there are 12 lunar cycles in a year, they associated a constellation with each cycle, one that was always in the same part of the sky during that cycle. They then named these constellations after animals and gods. These constellations could be used to tell somewhat reliably what was about to happen with the weather, so we have the stars predicting the future. Astrology! They also believed that when a planet that represented a god gave bad omens, it meant that god was angry. They then attempted to appease it to protect the king and their nation, which meant they believed in a two-way interaction between the movements in the sky and the actions of humans.

The Chinese developed their own system of astrology, with twelve Zodiac signs based on animals representing the years in which they were born, and five elements. Confucius believed in astrology, saying, "Heaven sends down its good or evil symbols and wise men act accordingly." They believed that the stars and planets predicted the rise and fall of dynasties.

Astrology Brings Understanding

People today use astrology to understand their personality better and know what their strengths and weaknesses are. They can use horoscopes to know when there may be upcoming challenges or opportunities. Your response to your environment is determined by personality, and an important factor in your personality is your Zodiac sign and its corresponding quality and element. Therefore, astrology can explain how you will respond in certain situations. This understanding can be used to your advantage or, at the very least, help you to know that it's just the way you are.

For example, someone with the Fixed quality (Taurus, Leo, Scorpio, Aquarius) will often be uncomfortable in times of great change in their life. They could use this knowledge to realize why they are upset and then strive to regain a routine in life. Astrology offers certain psychological insights that are the accumulation of centuries of knowledge. These can be a powerful help in times of uncertainty.

It is important to remember to act decisively when faced with good fortune or looming catastrophe. The planets and stars will not live your life for you, however much they may influence your life. If you do not use the knowledge astrology provides, you have gained nothing.

Using Astrology in Personal Relationships

As it is a matter of great importance to many people, astrology has become highly refined in providing knowledge about significant others. Horoscopes often include advice or predictions involving your lover or crush. You can use your Zodiac sign in dating to have an idea ahead of time how a relationship would work with someone, based on their Zodiac sign and how yours interacts with it. You can even use astrology as a pickup line: "Hey, beautiful! What's your sign?"

The relationship between two signs may be likely to work out because of shared interests and personality. Or it could be a cause for conflict, breeding misunderstanding and resentments. However, a good matchup between signs is no guarantee of a successful relationship, nor is a bad matchup a sure omen of a doomed one. Understanding your partner's astrological traits can help you to understand why your partner sees things and reacts to things the way they do. This can lead to more joyful times for both and it can help when working through conflicts. These sign interactions are a general guide to be used with consideration of other factors.

Astrology is helpful when it comes to interacting with your family. Understanding the characteristics of the signs for each of your family members can give insight on their words and deeds. You can learn about why there may be chronic conflict between two family members. You can use it to see an issue from the other point of view, which tends to decrease frustration and hostility. Reading horoscopes to family members can be a fun bonding activity.

For friends, astrology can be used to seek out the friendships most likely to succeed and to know why conflict arises and when that conflict may be irreconcilable, signaling it's time to move on. It can be used to understand the different mindsets of your friends and to know which ones would be best to undertake a project or go on a trip with.

Some signs have very different priorities and knowing and accepting the differences in your friend's motivations can be therapeutic. It can be very discouraging when you are excited about an idea and a friend shoots it down. It may be for a good reason, or it might be just because they have a different sign and mindset. In this case, it's best to share the idea with a friend of a more compatible sign.

ELEMENTS IN ASTROLOGY

The ancient Greeks believed that the world was composed of four elements: fire, earth, air, and water. Everything was a mixture of different amounts of these four elements. These four basic elements are no longer believed to be building blocks of our world, but they remain significant in astrology. In the same way that it was believed objects were composed of the four elements, it is now believed in astrology that the four elements make up our personalities. Each element has certain personality traits, and each sign has a unique mixture of these traits.

"China's Five Elements Philosophy" on chinahighlights.com explains that elements were first associated with zodiac signs in China in the Spring and Autumn period between 770 and 476 BC. Their zodiac signs are different animals, such as pig, rat, and dragon. They had five elements in traditional Chinese astrology: wood, water, earth, fire and metal. Each element was associated with 2 zodiac animals, except for Earth, which was attached to 4. As astrology spread from Asia and developed in Europe, each of the four ancient Greek elements became associated with 3 of the 12 zodiac signs.

Every person has an element, based on what their zodiac sign is.

The Air signs are Aquarius, Libra and Gemini.

The Water signs are Cancer, Pisces and Scorpio.

The Fire signs are Leo, Sagittarius and Aries.

The Earth signs are Capricorn, Virgo and Taurus

Your element affects you in many ways. It indicates certain personality traits that you have and explains how you will handle different situations. Your element is compatible with certain elements, so knowing your element can help you to find friends and lovers who are more likely to get along with you. Your element says a lot about what your strengths and weaknesses are and what kind of person you are. You can use this knowledge to play to your strengths and watch out for your weaknesses.

AIR

People whose sign is attached to the air element are intellectual; logical rather than emotional. They are witty, clever, and outgoing. They are excellent communicators because of their precise thinking. Because they are less reliant on emotion, they can remain calm and calculating in stressful situations.

They are most compatible with air, fire, and earth elements. They can have trouble with people of the water element because of the conflict between their calm logic and water's strong emotion. To bridge this gap, they need to speak the other's language, the language of feelings.

The heavy thinking that comes with the air element can be good or bad. With the Gemini, it causes indecisiveness due to over-analyzing things, but this prevents rash decisions. With the Aquarius, it means thinking about making things better far in the future, but this can cause their head to be in the clouds at times that require practicality. For the Libra, much of the thinking is about other people, but this can be expressed in either empathetic thoughts, or worrying about what other will think of them. Those with the air element would do well to remember that the world is not inside their head and that not everyone thinks as much as they do. However, their powers of intelligence are sure to serve them well in life.

WATER

Those whose sign connects with the water element are adaptable, emotional, and sensitive. They are deep and creative and they have great powers of imagination. They are in tune with the feelings of others and their observant qualities allow them to catch the subtle cues that a person in distress displays. They can be possessive and their knowledge of others emotions can be used for either nurture or manipulation.

The water element is most compatible with water and earth. For those of a water element dealing with people of the fire element, they should wear a thick skin and be ready to not take the fire element's occasional bursts of anger personally. They must remember that fire is impulsive and be patient with these people.

Those who are defined by the water element have strong emotions, and emotions can be powerful and difficult to control. However, emotion is a guiding force in our lives and shows us how to react to different circumstances.

A Cancer is loyal and very emotionally attached to their family, which is why it is good to be closely associated with a Cancer. A Cancer may overreact to perceived insults to their loved ones because they are so protective. The Pisces is friendly and altruistic, and rarely judgmental, but this faith in humanity may lead to them being taken advantage of, which causes many a Pisces to become depressed. Pisces are prone to sadness, but this also gives them an insight into the suffering of others, creating empathy with those in need. The Scorpio is brave and passionately attached to what they believe to be true. This can cause them to fight for something good, or if they are mistaken in their beliefs, to be a powerful force for evil. Their suspicious nature can protect them, but also make them paranoid, and therefore emotionally unstable.

Those with water as their element can overcome any weaknesses associated with emotionality by taking a time-out from the situation. A powerful emotion is like a strong fire, very hot, but quick to burn its fuel and end.

FIRE

Which brings us to the fire element! Those whose signs are attached to the fire element are energetic, impulsive, and enthusiastic. Their liveliness is inspiring and they make great leaders because of their charisma. They can also be very unpredictable and have a temper; they will be forceful when triggered. Adventurous and quick to try new things, people of the fire element are often groundbreakers and innovators. They stick with what their gut tells them and are very decisive.

Fire people are most compatible with air and fire people. When they deal with those of the earth element, they may become irritated with how grounded and practical they are and consider them boring. In this case, a fire person should keep their ego in check and realize that stable people are just as necessary as the impulsive ones.

The energy and charisma of people under the fire element can lead to a wide variety of outcomes. For the Aries, their energy is expressed in their speed and competitiveness. This impatience can lead to greatness, or frustration and anger. They always want to be first, and although they are very organized, their tendency to race through things can trip them up. For the Leo, their charisma leads to unparalleled leadership abilities. But they can also have a large ego and be stubborn and self-centered. Their ability to get their way from others means they might not address these issues, because they won't need to. When it comes to the Sagittarius, part of their charm is their uncompromising honesty. Their trustworthiness attracts people, but it can also drive them away if a Sagittarius says something brutally honest that hurts someone's feelings.

EARTH

The people whose sign is associated with the earth element can truly be described as down-to-earth. They are practical, emotionally stable, and reliable. They are not risk-takers nor are they prone to idealistic ambitions. Instead, they are focused on steadily making improvements in their lives and the lives of those they love. They are materialistic and intent on accumulating money and property.

Earth gets along best with earth and water. To get along with the fire element, earth people shouldn't try to save these impulsive risk-takers from failure, because they won't listen.

The stability and materialism of the earth element has predictable results. The Taurus is reliable yet stubborn and will be conservative in their life choices. They are good at making money, but they can also become greedy because of money's addictive properties. The Virgo does things systematically and never leaves anything undone. They are highly organized but this means they are prone to perfectionism. They can be judgmental of anyone who lacks their attention to detail, which may hurt someone's feelings. The Capricorn is disciplined and self-reliant. They are fond of tradition and value experience over experiment. Their commitment to tradition can lead to stubbornness and they often expect innovations to fail. Their faith in the tried and true can be utterly unshakeable.

ASTROLOGICAL QUALITY

In Astrology, there are 12 signs of the Zodiac. Each of these signs corresponds to one of three qualities: Cardinal, Fixed or Mutable. The qualities are also called quadruplicities because they each describe four of the Zodiac signs. Each quality has certain characteristics that correspond to the position in the season of the zodiac sign. The Zodiac signs that begin each season have the Cardinal quality, or "initiating energy". The Zodiac Signs in the middle of each season have the Fixed quality, or "maintaining energy". Finally, the Zodiac signs at the end of each season have the Mutable quality, or "changing energy".

Your quality says a lot about you and is an important addition to the self-knowledge astrology can provide. A person's quality determines both the inner energy of a person and how they respond to changes in their environment. It explains whether or not they are likely to change their opinions and how likely they are to be a leader or a follower. Knowing your quality can help you play to your strengths and realize what weak points in your energy you need to strengthen. Knowing where one needs improvement can be a path to greatness! Use this knowledge of qualities to achieve greater balance in your life.

Cardinal

At the beginning of each season are the four Zodiac signs with the Cardinal qualities: Aries, Cancer, Libra and Capricorn. These signs usher in the new season and get its momentum started up. Accordingly, people with the Cardinal quality love to start new things; they are innovators and trailblazers. They tend to be ambitious and energetic, eager to start new things. They seem to have endless drive towards accomplishing things, but they often don't finish what they start, because they get so excited about something new that they move on to that!

To go along with their ambition, those with the Cardinal quality can also have a large ego. A big ego is sometimes assumed to be a bad thing, but large egos come with confidence and the self-assuredness of leadership. They want to be the best at everything and work hard to get there. They are creative-types and innovators; trendsetters that the crowd will follow. However, they can be erratic due to their constant shifting of goals, and leaving things undone can cause problems.

Those with the Cardinal quality need to focus on finishing what they start. This may mean delaying a new project they are excited about in order to finish an older one. They can also surround themselves with people of the Fixed quality who will help them reach the finish line in all the races they start. It is very important that Cardinal quality people learn to finish their projects because of how valuable what they begin to create is!

Fixed

In the middle of each season are the four Zodiac signs with the Fixed quality: Leo, Taurus, Aquarius and Scorpio. If we compare those with the Cardinal quality to the hare who takes a nap because he is so far ahead in "The Tortoise and the Hare", we can say that those with the Fixed quality are like the tortoise. They prove that slow and steady wins the race. They have an innate ability to focus and stay committed. They are determined to reach their goals and will be persistent when faced with obstacles. People with the Fixed quality are the ones who get the job done, no matter how difficult or long the journey may be.

Fixed quality people prefer a predictable routine. Once they come to accept an idea or way of thinking, it is very hard or even impossible to get them to change their belief. This can be a strength, such as when they have an important moral belief that those around them have abandoned. It can also be a weakness when they refuse to adapt to new information. Fixed quality people are self-reliant but stubborn.

The best way for Fixed people to overcome their weakness is to open their mind and realize that they do not know everything. The entire universe is not already in their head and they need to be ready to accept new things. There is a Buddhist saying, "You cannot fill a cup that is already full." In this context, this means that when a Fixed person's mind is filled with beliefs that they won't let go of, there's no room to allow new beliefs to come in. Anyone with the Fixed quality should welcome the experience of being proven wrong and take advantage of the opportunity for growth that it offers.

Mutable

At the end of each season are the four Zodiac signs with the Mutable quality: Gemini, Virgo, Sagittarius and Pisces. These signs come at the end of the season, when weather is changing to make way for the new season. That's why the Mutable quality is the quality of change and adaptation. People who are Mutable are quick to follow the crowd and adapt to changes in their environment. This adaptability is extremely important for times of radical change; while those who are stuck in their ways are having problems, the Mutable people will already be back in stride.

Mutable quality people can be shallow, with no deep attachments to any principle, idea or way of life. This can be useful, as some people allow their beliefs to prevent them from seizing an advantage. Being opportunistic and flip-flopping has gotten plenty people ahead in life. However, doing so might get a Mutable person called out on their lack of commitment to ideals which others take very seriously. If they get caught acting different ways with different people, they will lose trust and rumors may spread.

The best way for Mutable people to make up for this weakness is to think for themselves. It's no shame to have other people's thoughts in one's head and be strongly influenced by trends; absolutely none of us are original in everything we think and say. However, the Mutable quality people need to find some time to be on their own and then decide what they think. Then they should take this out into the world and stick with it. No matter what your beliefs are, not everyone will agree with them, and that's okay. Not everyone has to be like you, or even like you!

RULING PLANETS: LIBRA

Every Zodiac sign has a ruling planet. The planets are large bodies orbiting the Sun and in astrology they are believed to strongly affect the lives of humans on Earth. The exact scientific definition of "planet" differs from astrology's. For astrology, the moon and the sun are considered planets because they are large bodies in our solar system. The planets alter our destiny and interpreting their movements is one of the main functions of astrology. The position of the ruling planet for your Zodiac sign is a major part of determining your horoscope.

Where do ruling planets come from?

The idea that ruling planets are associated with people born at certain times originated with the Romans. They divided the calendar year into portions associated with heavenly bodies. The Earth was once thought to be the center of the universe. So, when the planets moved backwards and forwards in the sky, or moved faster or slower, they didn't understand that it was because of the Earth's movement. They thought the planets were trying to communicate with humans. The same way observations of the stars predicted the seasons, they thought movements of planets predicted human destiny.

Eventually, Zodiac signs began to be associated with certain months, which led to the ruling planets for months turning into the ruling planets for Zodiac signs. Some signs share a ruling planet with another sign and some signs have two ruling planets, a new one and a classic one. Signs like Aquarius have two ruling planets (Uranus and Saturn) because for ancient astrologers, the furthest planet that they knew of was Saturn. When new planets were discovered, astrologers came to a consensus that some signs would be assigned to the newly discovered planets: Uranus, Neptune and Pluto. Their previous ruling planets are also considered significant, so these signs have two ruling planets.

Venus, Ruler of Libra

Venus was the goddess of love in Greek mythology, a beautiful woman who represented romantic desire. Libras are very romantically-inclined people who often have long-lasting love as their main goal in life. They desire the perfect romance and have the skills to get it. Those ruled by Venus appreciate human beauty even more than most and are often lusting after the most gorgeous men and women, whether they show it or not.

Venus also rules over all relationships and Libras are very sociable people. They are excellent at creating, repairing and maintaining relationships. They could be called diplomatic geniuses, because sometimes it seems like they can magically resolve even the fiercest of conflicts. They have a manner of speaking that deflates anger and a strong desire for everyone to get along, and when people pick up on that it sets them at ease.

Those ruled by Venus have a love of beauty, art and money. Libras are talented artists, writers, actors and musicians. They are also frequent visitors of art museums, where you can find them poring over the most sophisticated pieces. Many Libras use their artistic abilities to become wealthy because they are averse to hard labor. Libras have excellent taste in fashion, so expect to see a wealthy Libra on the cutting-edge of the fashion world. Even on the lowest of budgets a Libra will look amazing, and all Libras are willing to give fashion advice to anyone who asks!

SUN SIGN LIBRA

Libras are very diplomatic and social people. This zodiac sign is represented by the scales of justice. Their dislike of conflict makes them the greatest peacemakers in the zodiac. Libras are an Air sign and have the Cardinal quality. They are very intelligent but can have serious problems with applying themselves and doing hard work. Libras are some of the friendliest people in the world though, and use their social powers well to make up for their weaknesses.

Libra is an Air Sign

Libras are great thinkers and love to work out their ideas with other people. Libras are seldom stubborn in a debate and are some of the rare people who are willing to change their opinion after hearing the other side of it. They are perceptive of others and have a knack for remembering details about them. This in-depth knowledge of people is useful when they are trying to solve conflicts, because they can anticipate people's reactions.

Libras are very polite and it is hard to get mad at them, because of how even-headed they can be in the midst of a fight. A Libra knows just what to say to defuse the tension. Unscrupulous Libras will even use this talent to manipulate people who have a legitimate reason to be angry with them. However, it's more likely that a Libra will be using their diplomatic powers honorably, because even seeing someone else as the recipient of anger makes them uncomfortable.

Libras' ability and desire to keep the peace often means they appear indecisive, like they have no opinion of their own. It can seem like they're going back and forth between supporting different sides, when each side just wants someone to agree unconditionally with them. This is the Air element working in the Libra though; their opinions are based on facts, and in an argument, new facts about subjective states in people are coming in constantly. When a Libra suggests a compromise that seems like they've made no decision to people who demand to be declared right, they are demonstrating an intellectual strength, not indecisiveness.

Libra has the Cardinal Quality

Libras are great at coming up with ideas and have a lot of ambition. They will easily assemble a team to accomplish a task or project, but when it comes time to do the hard work, you might just find them making excuses, or not be able to find them at all. Libras compensate for this weakness by being the social glue that keeps a team together and making sure all the right people are involved. Libras can certainly finish the projects they start, but only if they get someone else to do a lot of the work.

Libras have a natural energy and they will strike up conversations with anyone and everyone. They will also take discussions in exciting new directions by coming up with cool new topics, or an innovative way to think about a subject. Libras like to learn about a lot of new things, but will not follow up on most of them. However, this habit of trying everything out leads to them discovering what they're truly passionate about and talented at, something many never find out because of a lack of exploration. This is why you'll rarely find an unfulfilled Libra in a career they don't want to be in.

Libra Likes

What's most important to a Libra is partnership. They want a significant other that they can show affection to and be in a stable relationship with. Libras like harmony and balance in a relationship, which means they want someone who can counter their weaknesses and excesses, yet still think like them and get along with them. Libras enjoy the challenge that comes with making things work in a relationship and they like that they can find compromises easily and naturally. Successfully making a relationship last through love and diplomacy is what a Libra likes most of all.

Libras love knowing all the facts of a situation, including facts about everyone involved. This is what allows them to make such great judgments; they will not be persuaded by their emotions. During disagreements they like finding the perfect solution that will make everyone happy. They like creating the perfect proposal and offer that appeals to every person involved. They get great satisfaction after fights from knowing that had they not been there, physical and emotional harm may have been done.

Libra Dislikes

What Libras dislike most is unfairness and injustice. They don't like it when they or others are cheated, overpowered or disregarded in any situation. They are smart enough to find a solution but they never like being reminded that the world can be such an unfair place. No Libra wants to see the weaker person lose unfairly and the stronger person get away with it, and if a Libra can do something about it, they will. Libras don't like liars, especially since their just and trusting nature can make them easy prey for deceitful people. False information compromises their excellent decision-making abilities and Libras despise that.

Libras don't like violence and will very rarely be violent themselves. Violence interferes with people's ability to get along and move on after an argument, because people tend to hold grudges when they're hit. Libras don't like when emotional wounds can't be healed. Libras don't like witnessing rivalries and grudges between people, especially when they're long-term ones and neither party is open to listening to a Libra's ideas for a solution. Libras are very against racism; it appalls them that someone would want to be rude to certain people before they even get to know them!

_____

_____

_____

_____

_____

_____

_____

_____

_____

_____

_____

_____

_____

_____

Libra

_____

_____

_____

_____

_____

CONNECT WITH US!

We'd love to connect with you so please visit the website or like us on Facebook!

Website:

www.MyTimeToColor.com

Facebook:

http://Facebook.com/mytimetocolor

POST A REVIEW

Your review means a lot so please consider taking a moment and posting a review on Amazon. Thanks!!

www.ingramcontent.com/pod-product-compliance
Lightning Source LLC
Chambersburg PA
CBHW082350220526
45470CB00008B/2703